For Roger

The publishers are grateful to the following for permission to use copyright material in this edition:

The Spangled Pandemonium by Palmer Brown from Beyond the Paw Paw Trees: The Story of Anna Lavinia by Palmer Brown. Copyright, 1954, by Palmer Brown.
Cheeky Little Skeleton © 1987 Lorraine Simeon.
The Bat by Colin West from Not to be Taken Seriously and The Small Ghostie by Barbara Ireson from Rhyme Time copyright © 1987 published by Century Hutchinson Publishing Group Ltd.
The Twitchetty Witch by Lilian Boucher from Is a Caterpillar Ticklish? collected by Adrian Rumble © 1986 published by Robert Royce Ltd, an imprint of Cassell plc.
The Alphabet Monster from Don't Eat Spiders by Robert Heidbreder, copyright © Robert Heidbreder 1985 (Toronto: Oxford University Press Canada, 1985); used by permission of the publisher.
Haunted House, Ghost and The Goblin by Jack Prelutsky from It's Hallowe'en copyright © 1977 Jack Prelutsky.
The Slitheree-Dee by Shel Silverstein © 1962 and 1968 Hollis Music, Inc., New York, assigned to TRO Essex Music Ltd.
International copyright secured. All rights reserved. Used by Permission.
My Other Granny by Ted Hughes from Meet My Folks by Ted Hughes, reprinted by permission of Faber and Faber Ltd.
I Left My Head by Lilian Moore from See My Lovely Poison Ivy copyright © 1975 Lilian Moore. All rights reserved. Reprinted by permission of Marian Reiner for the author.
The Hidebehind and **I'm Alone in the Evening** by Michael Rosen from Mind Your Own Business copyright © 1974 published by André Deutsch Ltd.
The Ugstabuggle by Peter Wesley-Smith from The Ombley Gombley © 1969 Peter Wesley-Smith and David Fielding, published by Angus & Robertson Publishers.
Monster and **Our Pond** by Richard Edwards from The Word Party copyright © 1986 Richard Edwards.
The Marrog by R.C. Scriven from Ducks and Dragons published by Faber and Faber, reprinted by permission of Harvey Unna and Stephen Durbridge Ltd.
The Bad Dream from Smile, Please! by Tony Bradman (Kestrel Books, 1987) p. 80.
Something is There by Lilian Moore from Spooky Rhymes and Riddles. Text copyright © 1972 by Lilian Moore. Reprinted by permission of Scholastic Inc.
hist whist by e.e. cummings is reprinted from Tulips and Chimneys by e.e. cummings, edited by George James Firmage, by permission of Liveright Publishing Corporation. Copyright 1923, 1925 and renewed 1951, 1953 by e.e. cummings. Copyright © 1973, 1976 by the Trustees for the e.e. cummings Trust. Copyright © 1973, 1976 by George James Firmage.
What's That? by Florence Parry Heide from My Sand Monster Poems copyright © 1976 by Florence Parry Heide reprinted by permission of Curtis Brown Ltd.
The Witch! The Witch! by Eleanor Farjeon from Silver and Snow published by Michael Joseph.

Text selection copyright © by Jill Bennett
Illustrations copyright © by Mary Rees

FIRST U.S. EDITION

First published in 1989
in Great Britain by
William Heinemann Ltd.

Library of Congress Catalog Card Number 89–83659

ISBN 0-316-08987-7

10 9 8 7 6 5 4 3 2 1

Ivy Street Books are
published by Little, Brown
and Company (Inc.)

Produced by Mandarin Offset
Printed and bound in Hong Kong

Spooky Poems

Collected by Jill Bennett

Pictures by Mary Rees

Little, Brown and Company
Boston · Toronto · London

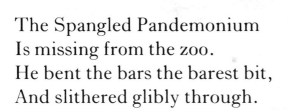

The Spangled Pandemonium
Is missing from the zoo.
He bent the bars the barest bit,
And slithered glibly through.

He crawled across the moated wall,
He climbed the mango tree,
And when his keeper scrambled up,
He nipped him in the knee.

To all of you, a warning
Not to wander after dark,
Or if you must, make very sure
You stay out of the park.

For the Spangled Pandemonium
Is missing from the zoo,
And since he nipped his keeper,
He would just as soon nip you!

Palmer Brown

THE HAIRY TOE

Once there was a woman went out to pick beans,
and she found a Hairy Toe.
She took the Hairy Toe home with her,
and that night, when she went to bed,
the wind began to moan and groan.
Away off in the distance
she seemed to hear a voice crying,
"Who's got my Hair-r-ry To-o-oe?
Who's got my Hair-r-ry To-o-oe?"

The woman scrooched down,
'way down under the covers,
and about that time
the wind appeared to hit the house,
smoosh,
and the old house creaked and cracked
like something was trying to get in.
The voice had come nearer,
almost at the door now,
and it said,
"Where's my Hair-r-ry To-o-oe?
Who's got my Hair-r-ry To-o-oe?"

The woman scrooched further down
under the covers
and pulled them tight around her head.

The wind growled around the house
like some big animal
and r-r-um-mbled
over the chimbley.
All at once she heard the door cr-r-a-ack
and Something slipped in
and began to creep over the floor.

The floor went
cre-e-eak, cre-e-eak
at every step that thing took towards her bed.
The woman could almost feel
it bending over her bed.
Then in an awful voice it said:
"Where's my Hair-r-ry To-o-oe?
Who's got my Hair-r-ry To-o-oe?"

You've got it!"

trad. American

THE BAT

The bat in flight at dead of night
Can flap about with ease,
For with his ears he somehow steers
A path between the trees.

Colin West

THE TWITCHETTY WITCH

A Twitchetty Witch
Went hurtling by,
Twitchetty, Witchetty,
Yooo-hooo-hooo!
Up in the dark
Where the black bats fly,
With her pointed nose
And her glittering eye,
A Twitchetty Witch
Went hurtling by,
Twitchetty, Witchetty –
S-w-w-i-i-i-s-shh!

Lilian Boucher

THE ALPHABET MONSTER

I'm the Alphabet Monster
And nothing tastes better
To the Alphabet Monster
Than eating a letter.
A "j" and an "a"
And a "c" and a "k"
And the million more letters
I munch every day.

I'm hungry now.
What shall I do?
I think I'll eat
a "y"
an "o"
and a "u"

That means . . . YOU!

Robert Heidbreder

HAUNTED HOUSE

There's a house upon the hilltop
We will not go inside
For that is where the witches live,
Where ghosts and goblins hide.

Tonight they have their party,
All the lights are burning bright,
But oh we will not go inside
The haunted house tonight.

The demons there are whirling
And the spirits swirl about.
They sing their songs to Hallowe'en.
"Come join the fun," they shout.

But we do not want to go there
So we run with all our might
And oh we will not go inside
The haunted house tonight.

Jack Prelutsky

THE SLITHEREE-DEE

The Slitheree-dee has crawled out of the sea;
He may catch all the others, but he won't catch me.
No, you won't catch me, old Slitheree-dee;
You may catch all the others, but you wo . . .

Shel Silverstein

MY OTHER GRANNY

My Granny is an Octopus
At the bottom of the sea,
And when she comes to supper
She brings her family.

She chooses a wild wet windy night
When the world rolls blind
As a boulder in the night-sea surf,
And her family troops behind.

Ted Hughes

I LEFT MY HEAD

I left my head
somewhere
today.

Put it down for
just
a minute.

Under the
table?
On a chair?

Wish I were
able
to say
where.

Everything I need
is
in it!

Lilian Moore

THE HIDEBEHIND

Have you seen the Hidebehind?
I don't think you will, mind you,
because as you're running through the dark
the Hidebehind's behind you.

Michael Rosen

THE UGSTABUGGLE

Over by my bedroom wall
The Ugstabuggle stands,
A monster nearly nine feet tall
With hairy, grasping hands.
In afternoons and mornings
He's always out of sight,
But often I can see him
In the darkness late at night.
Yet when I do not think of him
He disappears again,
And when I sleep he goes, because
I cannot see him then!

Peter Wesley-Smith

THE MARROG

My desk's at the back of the class
And nobody, nobody knows
I'm a Marrog from Mars
With a body of brass
And seventeen fingers and toes.

Wouldn't they shriek if they knew
I've three eyes at the back of my head
And my hair is bright purple
My nose is deep blue
And my teeth are half-yellow, half-red

My five arms are silver, and spiked
With knives on them sharper than spears.
I could go back right now, if I liked—
And return in a million light-years.

I could gobble them all,
For I'm seven foot tall
And I'm breathing green flames from my ears.

Wouldn't they yell if they knew,
If they guessed that a Marrog was here?
Ha-ha, they haven't a clue—
Or wouldn't they tremble with fear!
"Look, look, a Marrog"
They'd all scream—and SMACK
The blackboard would fall and the ceiling would crack

And teacher would faint, I suppose.
But I grin to myself, sitting right at the back
And nobody, nobody knows.

R. C. Scriven

MONSTER

I saw a monster in the woods
As I was cycling by,
His footsteps smouldered in the leaves,
His breath made bushes die,

And when he raised his hairy arm
It blotted out the sun;
He snatched a pigeon from the sky
And swallowed it in one.

His mouth was like a dripping cave,
His eyes like pools of lead,
And when he growled I rode back home
And rushed upstairs to bed.

But that was yesterday and though
It gave me quite a fright,
I'm older now and braver so
I'm going back tonight.

I'll tie him up when he's asleep
And take him to the zoo.
The trouble is he's rather big . . .
Will you come too?

Richard Edwards

SOMETHING IS THERE

Something is there
there on the stair
coming down
    coming down
        stepping with care.
Coming down
    coming down
        slinkety-sly.

Something is coming and wants to get by.

Lilian Moore

I'M ALONE IN THE EVENING

I'm alone in the evening
when the family sits
reading and sleeping
and I watch the fire in close
to see flame goblins
wriggling out of their caves
for the evening

I'm alone

when mum's switched out the light
my head against the pillow
listening to a ca-thump ca-thump
in the middle of my ears.
It's my heart.

Michael Rosen

THE BAD DREAM

Sleep . . . deep.
Night . . . FRIGHT!
Dream . . . SCREAM!
Mum . . . comes.
"There, there . . ."
Kiss, kiss . . .
Thumb . . . mmmmm.
"Night, night . . .
Sleep tight . . ."
Sleep . . . deep . . .

Tony Bradman

hist   whist
little ghostthings
tip-toe
twinkle toe

little twitchy
witches and tingling
goblins
hob-a-nob

hob-a-nob

little hoppy happy
toad in tweeds
tweeds
little itchy mousies

with scuttling
eyes   rustle and run and
hidehidehide
whisk

whisk   look out for the old woman
with the wart on her nose
what she'll do to yer
nobody knows

for she knows the devil   ooch
the devil   ouch
the devil
ach   the great

green
dancing
devil
devil

devil
devil

wheeEEE

e. e. cummings

OUR POND

The pond in our garden
Is murky and deep
And lots of things live there
That slither and creep.

Like diving bell spiders
And great ramshorn snails
And whirligig beetles
And black snappertails.

There used to be goldfish
That nibbled my thumb,
But now there's just algae
And sour, crusty scum.

There used to be pondweed
With fizzy green shoots,
But now there are leeches
And horrible newts.

One day when my football
Rolled in by mistake
I tried to retrieve it
By using a rake,

But as I leaned over
A shape from the ooze
Bulged up like a nightmare
And lunged at my shoes.

I ran back in shouting.
But everyone laughed
And said I was teasing
Or else I was daft.

But I know what happened
And when I'm asleep
I dream of those creatures
That slither and creep.

Richard Edwards

THE GOBLIN

There's a goblin as green
As a goblin can be
Who is sitting outside
And is waiting for me.
When he knocked on my door
And said softly, "Come play!"
I answered, "No thank you,
Now please, go away!"
But the goblin as green
As a goblin can be
Is still sitting outside
And is waiting for me.

Jack Prelutsky

GHOST

I saw a ghost
that stared and stared
And I stood still
and acted scared.

But that was just
a big pretend.

I knew that ghost . . .

. . . it was my friend!

Jack Prelutsky

THE SMALL GHOSTIE

When it's late and it's dark
And everyone sleeps . . . shhh shhh shhh,
Into our kitchen
A small ghostie creeps . . . shhh shhh shhh.

We hear knockings and raps
And then rattles and taps,

Then he clatters and clangs
And he batters and bangs,

And he whistles and yowls
And he screeches and howls . . .

So we pull up our covers over our heads
And we block up our ears and WE STAY IN OUR BEDS.

Barbara Ireson

CHEEKY LITTLE SKELETON

I was sitting in the bath one day
when in walked a skeleton.
He hadn't any clothes on
but he wore a pair of wellingtons.
I looked at him and he looked at me,
he said, I'm coming in to get you.
One, two, three.

He dived into the bath with me,
I couldn't stand the sight of him.
I knew that I was trapped so
I agreed to fight with him.
He hadn't any muscles and he wasn't very strong,
pulling him to pieces
didn't take me very long.

As I stepped out of the bath,
he began to speak to me.
If I put him back together
there'd be a special treat for me.
Put me back together, boy, and watch me disappear.
He looked awfully untidy,
bones were lying everywhere.

So I put him back together,
that cheeky little skeleton.
As quiet as a mouse he sat,
as I slipped on his wellingtons.
I looked at him and he looked at me,
he said, I'm gonna have to leave you, boy,
One, two, three.

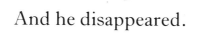

And he disappeared.

Lorraine Simeon

WHAT'S THAT?

What's that?
Who's there?
There's a great huge horrible *horrible*
creeping up the stair!
A huge big terrible *terrible*
with creepy crawly hair!
There's a ghastly grisly *ghastly*
with seven slimy eyes!
And flabby grabby tentacles
of a gigantic size!
He's crept into my room now,
he's leaning over me.
I wonder if he's thinking
how delicious I will be.

Florence Parry Heide

I know a man
Who's back to front
The strangest man *I've* seen.
He can't tell where he's going
But he knows where he has been.

Spike Milligan

The Witch! the Witch! don't let her get you!

Or your Aunt wouldn't know you the next time
she met you!

Eleanor Farjeon